Hueber Lektüren

AF203851

Englisch

Merlin's Dragon

LEKTÜRE MIT AUDIOS ONLINE

Sue Murray

Illustrated by Paul Fisher Johnson

Hueber Verlag

This is the German version of **Merlin's Dragon**

Merlin's Dragon

ILTS Created and developed by
International Language Teaching Services Ltd
First floor, 1 Market Street
Saffron Walden, Essex CB10 1JB, UK

help@ilts.info
www.ilts.info

Author: Sue Murray
Series editor: James Bean
Illustrations: Paul Fisher Johnson
Text design: ILTS Ltd
Origination: e-BookServices.com
Audio production: Mike Raggett, Verbalists; Mark Smith, Tally Ho Studio
Voice actor: Wayne Forester

Der Verlag weist ausdrücklich darauf hin, dass im Text enthaltene externe Links vom Verlag nur bis zum Zeitpunkt der Buchveröffentlichung eingesehen werden konnten. Auf spätere Veränderungen hat der Verlag keinerlei Einfluss. Eine Haftung des Verlags ist daher ausgeschlossen.

3. 2. 1. | Die letzten Ziffern
2026 25 24 23 22 | bezeichnen Zahl und Jahr des Druckes.
Alle Drucke dieser Auflage können, da unverändert,
nebeneinander benutzt werden.
1. Auflage
Copyright © 2022 International Language Teaching Services Ltd
© 2022 Hueber Verlag GmbH & Co. KG, München, Deutschland
Umschlaggestaltung: Sieveking · Agentur für Kommunikation, München
Cover: © Miklos - stock.adobe.com; Seiten 4–5: Flagge Wales © Getty Images/
iStock/jmci; Bahn © Getty Images/iStock/Rixipix; Snowdonia-Nationalpark,
Besucherzentrum © Getty Images/iStock/Maisna; Wanderweg © Getty Images/
iStock/Aiselin82
Verlagsredaktion: Heike Birner, Hueber Verlag, München
Druck und Bindung: Friedrich Pustet GmbH & Co. KG, Regensburg
Printed in Germany
ISBN 978–3–19–262997–6

Art. 530_28574_001_01

Contents

▶ Das Hörbuch zur Lektüre und die Tracks zu den Übungen stehen als kostenloser MP3-Download bereit unter:
www.hueber.de/audioservice
Zugangscode: 5b5714f90z

SNOWDONIA

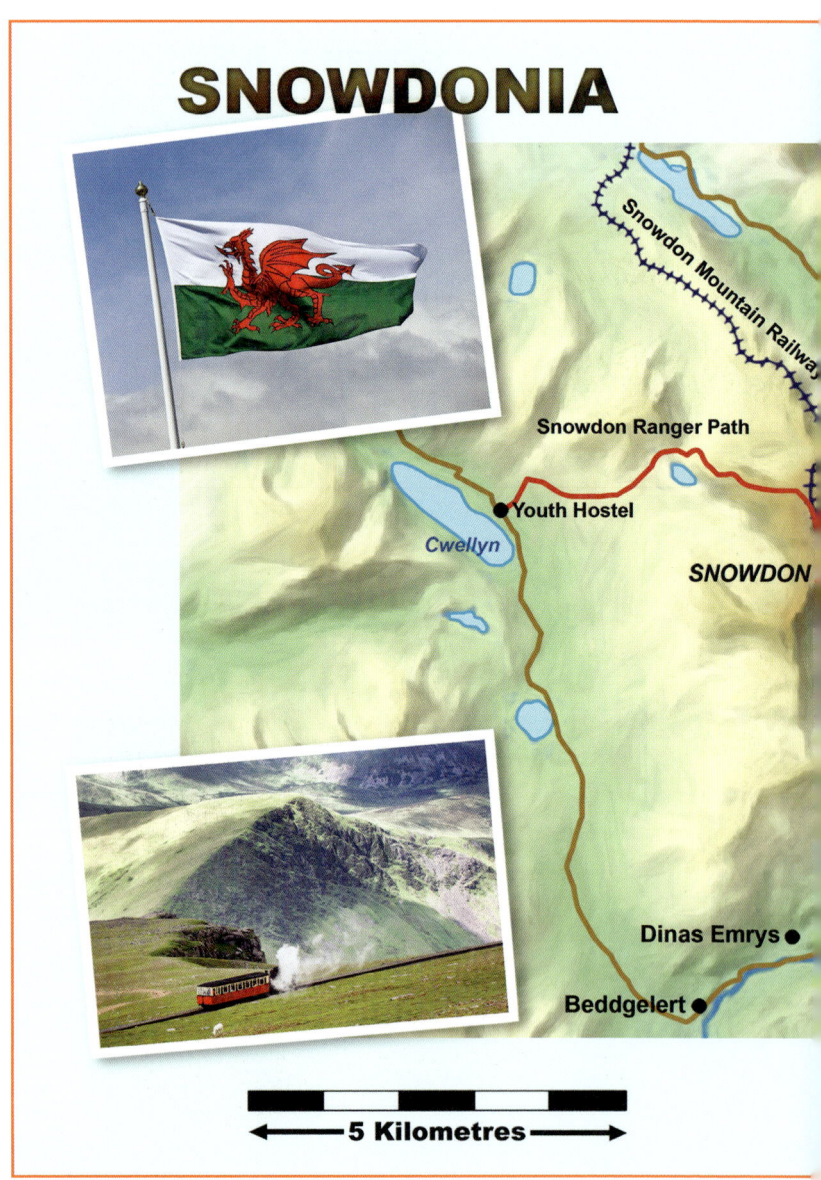

Snowdon Mountain Railway

Snowdon Ranger Path

●Youth Hostel

Cwellyn

SNOWDON

Dinas Emrys ●

Beddgelert ●

5 Kilometres

WALES

Pyg Track

● Pen - y - Pass

Llydaw

Y LLIWEDD

Gwynant

Chapter 1

A dragon sleeps here

'I see Snowdon!' says Parker. 'That mountain — it's Snowdon!'

Parker is with his family. They're driving in Snowdonia, a national park in Wales. It's a warm, sunny day in April. They are going to be in Snowdonia for three days.

'Oh yes! I see it too!' says his sister, Olivia. Parker is fourteen and Olivia is sixteen. 'Snowdon is 1085 metres tall.' Olivia is reading from a book, *Walking in Snowdonia National Park*.

'We'll be at Dinas Emrys in five minutes,' says their father, Frank. Frank is looking at a map of the national park.

'Good,' says their mother, Chris. She's driving. 'We can have lunch there.'

Parker's parents are archaeologists. Dinas Emrys is an ancient fort. Chris and Frank are going to work there.

'There's the car park,' says Frank.

Soon, the family are walking on the path to the fort. They all have their lunches in their backpacks. The path goes up ancient stone steps and through a big forest.

'There's a story in my book about this place, about Dinas Emrys,' says Parker. He takes a small book out of his backpack. 'The story is about Merlin, King Arthur's wizard. I love stories about Merlin and King Arthur. And I love stories about magic and dragons.'

'We know that!' says his mother.

Parker tells Olivia, 'Emrys is Merlin's other name.'

Frank says, 'And Dinas means fort.'

Olivia says, 'So, Dinas Emrys is ... the fort of Merlin!'

'It's good to be here,' says Parker. He looks up at Snowdon. 'Merlin's asleep up there. I know he is.'

'That's what the old stories say,' says his father.

They walk across a small bridge. There are two paths ahead of them.

'Where do we go now?' Chris asks.

Olivia looks at a map in her book. 'That way.'

They walk for thirty minutes. The path goes up a hill. They climb over a stone wall.

'We're here!' says Chris.

'Where's the fort?' asks Parker.

'This is it,' Frank answers. 'Look at these stones. Mum and I are going to photograph these ancient walls and stones.'

The family walk over and look at the ancient stones. They sit and eat their lunch.

'Wow, look at the view!' says Parker. 'It's a great place for a fort.'

They are at the top of a large hill. They can see mountains, fields, forests and a big lake.

Chris says, 'We're here! At Vortigern's fort.' She looks at Frank and smiles.

'Who is Vortigern?' Olivia asks.

'Ah! I know who he is,' says Parker. 'Vortigern is in my book. He's the king. At the start of the story, King Vortigern builds a fort. But the walls of his fort fall down every night. Vortigern must stop the walls from falling down. He asks his wizard for help. A lot of people are looking at the

stones. Merlin is there too. He's a boy, and people call him Emrys.'

Parker opens his book. He reads to his family:

Vortigern's wizard says, 'King Vortigern, there is bad magic here.'

'Bad magic?' the king says. 'I must stop it.'

'To stop the bad magic, you must kill a boy with no father,' the wizard tells Vortigern. The wizard looks at Merlin. 'You must kill this boy. Kill him, or your walls are going to fall down every night.'

Merlin looks at the king. 'I have no father, King Vortigern. But don't kill me. I can stop these walls from falling down every night. It's not bad magic,' Merlin says. 'It is dragons. There are two dragons under your fort: a red dragon and a white dragon. They are asleep now. They sleep every day. But they fight every night. Their fighting makes the walls fall down every night.'

'Kill the boy!' says the king's wizard.

'Dig here,' says Merlin. 'Wake up the dragons.'

Vortigern looks at his wizard and at the young boy.

'Dig!' says Vortigern to his men.

Parker closes his book. He says, 'And soon, everyone sees the two dragons. The dragons wake up. They fight. The red dragon wins. And that dragon is the red dragon of Wales. At the end of the story, Vortigern wants to thank young Merlin. He names this place Dinas Emrys!'

Chapter 2

The path to Snowdon

'I'm hungry,' says Parker. The family are driving beside a lake called Cwellyn.

Chris says, 'This is a pretty place.'

'Look for the Snowdon Ranger Youth Hostel,' says Frank. He's driving now.

'There it is!' says Parker.

Frank stops the car in front of the old stone building. Everyone gets their bags and backpacks out.

Inside, a large man with a beard smiles and says, 'Welcome to Snowdon Ranger Youth Hostel.'

'Hi,' says Chris. 'We're the Wentworths. I'm Chris, this is my husband Frank, and these are our children, Olivia and Parker.'

'Hello, everyone.' The man looks at his computer. 'Wentworth. Ah, yes, you're staying here for three nights. You're in Rooms Five and Six. I'm George. Do you have any questions? Ask me anything about the hostel or about Snowdonia.'

Olivia says, 'Great! Thanks, George. Can we walk to the top of Snowdon and back again in one day? My book says you can.'

'Are you a good walker, young woman?'

'We all are,' says Chris. 'But Frank and I will be working at Dinas Emrys. We're archaeologists. The children are going to go on some walks without us.'

Olivia says, 'Parker and I love going on long walks.'

Parker says, 'I'm going to look for Merlin's cave.'

George looks at Parker. 'Merlin's cave!'

'Yes,' says Parker. 'He's asleep in the hills here. I know he is.'

George smiles. 'I think he is too. I often go walking and then I look for Merlin's cave.'

'Is it okay for the children to walk up Snowdon without us, George?' Frank asks.

'Oh, yes,' George answers. 'Don't worry. It's not dangerous. Lots of people walk on the Snowdon Ranger Path every day. And the path is easy to see.' He looks at Parker and Olivia. 'Look at this map.'

George goes to a large map on the wall. 'This is Snowdonia. We are here.' He points to the map. 'You see this path? That's the Snowdon Ranger Path. You can walk from here to the top of Snowdon in three or four hours.'

'Great!' says Olivia. 'We can have lunch up there, and walk down the path again.'

'Yes,' George says. 'Or you can come down on the Pyg Track.' He points to a path that goes east from the top of Snowdon to a place called Pen-y-Pass. 'You can walk that track in three hours.'

'But can we get back here?' Parker asks. 'Is there a bus?'

George asks Chris and Frank, 'You're working at Dinas Emrys, aren't you?'

'Yes, we are,' Chris says.

'Good. It's a fifteen-minute drive from Dinas Emrys to Pen-y-Pass. You can meet the kids in the Pen-y-Pass car park in the afternoon. And you can stop at this village for dinner.' George points to a place named Beddgelert.

'Dinner! I'm hungry!' Parker says.

Everyone laughs.

George points to a door and says, 'The kitchen's that way.'

Soon, the family are sitting at the large dining table in the youth hostel's kitchen. They're having dinner.

'This curry is good,' says Parker. 'Thanks, Dad.'

'You're welcome,' says Frank. 'Olivia, is the weather going to be good tomorrow? What's the forecast?'

'It's going to be sunny but cold,' Olivia answers. 'Good weather for a long walk.'

'I worry about you two going without us,' Frank says. 'On mountains the weather can change in an hour. It can be dangerous up there.'

'Don't worry, Dad,' Parker says. 'We'll take warm clothes with us. And our rain jackets.'

'And we'll look at the forecast again in the morning,' Olivia says. 'And I have my phone. I can phone you any time.'

Chris says, 'It's good for the children to do this without us, Frank.'

'Okay,' says Frank. 'But I'll worry.'

'No, you won't, Dad,' says Olivia. 'Tomorrow, you'll be working on those ancient walls. You won't be thinking about us.'

Frank smiles. 'Yes, okay.'

'Tomorrow is going to be a great day!' Parker says.

Chapter 3

To the top

'Do you have your warm clothing?' Frank asks Olivia and Parker. It's nine o'clock in the morning. The family are standing outside the youth hostel.

'Yes, Dad,' answers Olivia. We have our jumpers, rain jackets, beanies, scarves and gloves.'

'And your food?'

'Yes, Dad,' says Parker. 'We have our sandwiches, fruit, nuts, water and our chocolate bars.'

Olivia says, 'And I have my map and my phone. We'll be okay.'

'It's a nice day for walking,' Chris says. 'Have a great day, you two. We'll see you at Pen-y-Pass at five o'clock.'

George comes out of the hostel. 'The forecast is okay,' he says. 'There's a storm over the Irish Sea, but it's not coming this way. But please watch the sky. The weather can change at any time. You can turn back and do the walk tomorrow.'

'Thanks, George. See you tonight!' Olivia says. 'Come on, Parker.' She walks across the road from the youth hostel to the start of the track.

'Hey, George,' Parker says. 'Maybe I'll find Merlin's cave today!'

George smiles. 'Yes, maybe. Look to the south, young man.'

'The south? Okay! Bye!' Parker says.

Soon, Parker and Olivia are on the Snowdon Ranger Path. It goes up a steep hill to a farm.

Olivia looks at the map in her book. 'The path is that way.' She points. 'Behind that farmhouse.'

'Look,' says Parker. On a rock beside a gate is the word PATH. 'George is right – the path is easy to see!'

The stone path goes up through green fields. Parker and Olivia walk for half an hour.

'Look at those clouds, Olivia,' says Parker. He points to the north. The clouds are thick and grey.

'That's the storm over the Irish Sea,' says Olivia. 'Don't worry.'

'I won't. But I'm going to watch the weather,' says Parker.

They walk along the track. At a gate, they see:

SNOWDON RANGER PATH TO SNOWDON SUMMIT – 4.6 KM

'We're two kilometres along the track already!' says Olivia. 'Let's stop for ten minutes.'

'Good! I'm hot!' says Parker. He gets out his water bottle.

'It's a warm morning,' says Olivia.

They sit on the stone wall and eat their fruit and nuts. They look at the clouds.

Olivia points to a cloud and says, 'I can see a cat!'

'Oh, yes,' says Parker. 'And look! I see a dragon! A grey dragon!'

Two people come through the gate, a man and a woman.

'Good morning,' says the woman.

'Hi,' says Parker. 'Are you coming back from the top of Snowdon already?'

'No,' says the man. 'We're turning back. Look at those clouds.'

The woman says, 'The weather is changing. A storm is coming.'

'Oh,' says Olivia, 'but the storms over the Irish Sea don't come this way. And the forecast is good. Look.' She points to the forecast on her phone.

The man looks at the forecast, and then at the sky. 'That storm is coming. Come back down with us.'

'Thanks, but we're okay,' says Olivia. 'We'll keep going.'

'Okay,' says the man. 'But be careful.'

The walkers go down the path.

Olivia and Parker go through the gate and walk up the steep path. They walk up and up for an hour.

At noon, a cold wind starts. Parker says to Olivia, 'Look at the clouds. They're dark now. I think it's time to go back.'

'But we're near the summit, Parker,' she says. 'You can look for Merlin's cave.'

'Phone Dad,' Parker says. 'Talk to him.'

Olivia looks at her phone. 'Uh oh. There's no signal here.'

'I'm cold,' says Parker.

The air is very cold now, and the sky is grey.

'It's time to put on your jumper, Parker,' says his sister.

'I'm putting on my jacket and gloves too – and my beanie!'

They put on all their warm clothes.

'Come on, Parker. Walk for fifteen more minutes,' Olivia says. 'We're near the summit.'

'Okay.' Parker looks to the south. The sky is blue there. 'Merlin's cave is down there.'

They come to a railway line. 'Ah, this is the Snowdon Railway line,' Olivia says. 'A train brings people up to the summit in the summer. But there's no train now.'

'There are no people here, Olivia, and that storm is close!' Parker says. 'And we can't phone Dad. It's cold. I want to go back.'

'But we're close to the summit! Look, we're here on the map. Come on, we can eat lunch on top of the mountain!'

'No, I'm going back.' Parker turns to go back down the track. 'Oh, no! Look, Olivia!'

She turns too. They see the storm coming. In minutes, Parker and Olivia can't see anything five metres away. They are in the storm clouds. And it's freezing.

Chapter 4

In the storm

'What are we going to do?' Parker asks.

'Don't worry,' Olivia answers. 'Storms come and go here. Come on – I can see the path to the summit.'

'Maybe you can get a phone signal up there. We must phone Dad. He's going to worry about this bad weather.'

The two of them walk along the path and up some big stone stairs. They are walking in thick mist.

'There!' Olivia says. 'The summit!'

Parker sees the stone marker at the summit. 'Let's sit behind this stone marker, out of the wind,' he says.

They sit with their backs on the marker.

'We're here!' Olivia says. 'We're at the top of Snowdon!'

'But we can't see anything,' Parker says. 'And it's freezing!'

'But we're here!' Olivia says again.

'Can you get a signal now?'

Olivia looks at her phone. 'No.'

'Where is east?' Parker says. He's looking at Olivia's map.

She looks into the mist and says, 'That way, I think.'

'Y Lliwedd is east of here. It's a mountain. In my book, King Arthur's knights are asleep in a cave on Y Lliwedd.'

'Maybe Merlin's asleep in that cave too,' Olivia says.

'I think his cave is near here, but maybe it's to the south. Or maybe Merlin's asleep below us now, here on Snowdon!'

It starts snowing.

'Oh, no,' Olivia says. 'Come on, Parker, we have to get out of the snow!'

'Where can we go?'

'There's a building near the summit – the Visitors Centre. The train stops there. It's not open now, but maybe we can get out of this bad weather. It's freezing here.'

'But where is the Visitors Centre? Where's the path?' Parker asks his sister. 'I can't see anything.'

The whole world is white – the sky and the ground.

'Oh, no!' Olivia stands up and puts on her backpack. 'It's this way, I think.'

But Olivia is walking on the icy ground. Her foot slips on the ice and she falls. 'Ow!' she says. 'My foot! Ow!'

'Olivia!' Parker goes over to her. 'Can you stand up?'

'No! It hurts!'

'We have to get to the Visitors Centre,' Parker says. 'We can't stay here in the snow. I'll look for it. I'll come back for you and take you there.'

'But you can't see where you're going! The mountain is dangerous. People die here. Don't go, Parker. Stay with me.'

'I won't be long,' Parker says. 'You stay here, behind the stones, out of the wind. Here, our backpacks can be a wall for you. And here's my chocolate bar.'

Soon, Parker is walking off into the storm.

'Be careful!' Olivia says.

I mustn't fall, he thinks. *I must help Olivia. I mustn't slip.*

Parker turns back but he can't see his sister. *Am I going the right way? Where's the track? Where are the stone stairs?*

Parker takes three small steps. He stops. He looks ahead but he can't see anything. It's snowing hard now and the wind is getting stronger and stronger.

The snow hurts his face. He closes his eyes. *The mountain is steep here. There are cliffs. I must not walk the wrong way. People die falling off these cliffs.*

Olivia's voice comes to him on the wind. 'Be careful, Parker!'

He shouts back, 'Yes, Olivia. Stay warm!'

Can she hear me? He takes two small steps. *I'm so cold. And so tired. What can I do?*

The sky is white. Parker's whole world is white. He can't move. *People die here. Am I going to die? Is Olivia going to die? Will we freeze to death? I must do something! But what?*

Then Parker calls into the wild wind, 'Merlin! Are you there? Merlin, help me! Wake up, Merlin! Send help, please! Merlin!' The wind carries his words away.

Parker takes one step, two steps. He sees a big red ball in the white sky. *Is that the sun?* he thinks. *No, it can't be. The clouds are too thick. What is it?*

He takes a step. The wind is strong now, coming from the north, the south, the east and the west. The wind is roaring at him.

Parker looks up again. Out of the clouds, he sees something flying towards him. Something big, something red.

It's not the wind roaring – it's a dragon!

The dragon roars. Hot flames shoot out of its mouth. The air is warm. The snow in front of Parker melts. He sees a cliff, three steps ahead!

The dragon roars again. More flames shoot out of its mouth. The air is warm again. The snow behind Parker melts.

The stairs! I can see the stone stairs!

Parker looks up, and calls out, 'Thank you!'

The dragon flies in a circle above Parker, then flies into the clouds.

The wind stops. The snow stops.

Parker stands on the cliff and calls out, 'Thank you, Merlin!'

Chapter 5

Goodbye for now

Parker goes back to Olivia.

'It's going to be okay, Olivia,' he says to his sister. 'We can see the path to the Visitors Centre now.'

'Great!' she says. 'Snow melts fast here.'

'Ah! You have to thank Merlin. He's listening. Merlin likes to help people. He sends his dragon – the red dragon of Wales. It can melt snow with its hot flames!'

'Oh, Parker – you and your dragons. There are no such things as dragons.'

'Oh yes, there are. But come on, we must get to the building. It's freezing out here.'

He picks up both backpacks. He puts on his backpack and carries Olivia's.

He helps Olivia to stand up and says, 'We won't go fast. The ground is still icy.'

Soon, they get to the Visitors Centre.

'We must get inside,' Olivia says. 'It's so cold.'

'And maybe there's a phone inside,' Parker says.

He tries to open the doors and the windows but he can't. He looks at Olivia. She looks very tired and ill.

'Wait here,' Parker says. He goes back to the path and picks up a large rock.

'What are you going to do?' asks Olivia.

'I'm going to break a window.'

'Parker. You can't!'

'We have to get inside, Olivia.' He breaks a window with the rock. 'Wait here.'

Parker goes through the window. Then he comes and opens the door for Olivia.

'There's a phone!' Parker says. He calls his father.

'Hello?' It's Chris, not Frank.

'Mum? Mum! Don't worry, Olivia and I are okay.'

Chris says, 'That's nice. Thanks for phoning, Parker. Things are good here too. Your father is taking a photograph of –'

'Mum! I'm calling to say that we're safe! The snow storm is not too bad now –'

'Snow storm? It's fine here at Dinas Emrys,' says Chris. 'Oh – yes, I can see the dark clouds up there on the mountain now. Huh.'

'Mum – Olivia's hurt. It's her foot. She can't walk. We can't get down from here,' Parker says. 'Can you please give the phone to Dad?'

'Parker, is that you? It's Dad. Tell me what's wrong.'

Soon, Olivia and Parker are sitting on a couch in the Visitors Centre. They are eating their sandwiches. They know that help is coming. It's snowing outside but they're warm and safe.

'Tell me again about Merlin and the dragons at Dinas Emrys,' Olivia asks her brother.

Then they see a bright red light in the sky.

'Is that lightning?' says Olivia.

Parker goes to the window. 'No! It's Merlin's dragon!'

His sister smiles and says, 'Oh, Parker!'

Parker calls out, 'I'm going to come back one day! Thank you! Goodbye!'

Activities

Chapter 1

Before you read

A. Look at the map on pages 4 and 5. Circle the correct answers.
1. Where is the youth hostel?
   a. on a mountain   b. near a lake   c. beside a railway line
2. From the youth hostel, where does the path go?
   a. to Snowdon   b. to Y Lliwedd   c. to the lake called Llydaw

B. Find these words in your dictionary. Use them in the sentences.
ancient   dragon   map   fort
1. On the hill there is an old _____ with high walls.
2. This town is _____. It's 2000 years old!
3. Where are we? Let's look at the _____.
4. I'm reading a story about a _____. It can fly, and fire comes from its mouth!

C. Listen to Track 3 and answer these questions.
1. Where is Snowdonia National Park?
   a. in Scotland   b. in Wales
2. How long will Parker's family be in Snowdonia?
   a. for three days   b. for fourteen days
3. How tall is Snowdon?
   a. 1085 metres   b. 1850 metres

After you read

COMPREHENSION

A. Circle the correct answers.
1. Frank and Chris both have the same job. What are they?
   a. teachers   b. archaeologists   c. writers
2. What are Frank and Chris going to do in Snowdonia?
   a. climb a mountain   b. visit friends   c. work at a fort
3. What is Dinas Emrys?
   a. a village   b. an ancient fort   c. a mountain
4. Where does the path to Dinas Emrys go?
   a. through a forest   b. beside a lake   c. across a field

B. Circle T for true or F for false for these sentences.
1. In Parker's book there is a story about Dinas Emrys.   T / F
2. Dinas is another name for Merlin.   T / F
3. Dinas Emrys is at the top of a hill.   T / F
4. Chris and Frank are going to photograph the walls
   and stones of Dinas Emrys.   T / F

C. Complete these sentences.
1. In the story in Parker's book, Vortigern is the _____.
2. Every night, the walls of the fort _____.
3. Vortigern asks for help from his _____.
4. In the story, Merlin is a boy called _____.

D. Write short answers to these questions.
1. What does the wizard tell Vortigern to do?
   _____

2. What sleeps under Vortigern's fort?
   _____

3. At night, what makes the walls fall down?
   _____

4. Which dragon wins the fight?
   _____

LANGUAGE ACTIVITIES
A. Match the words that go together in Chapter 1.
1. walk across   a map
2. walk up   a bridge
3. look at   a wall
4. climb over   a hill

B. Write the missing nouns in these phrases from Chapter 1.
1. a book of old _____   3. a boy with no _____
2. bad _____   4. the red dragon of _____

WHAT DO YOU THINK?
Parker loves stories about Merlin, King Arthur, magic and
dragons. Do you like stories like that? Why or why not?

_____

Chapter 2

Before you read

A. Look at the picture on page 12 and circle the correct answers.
1. What is the man showing to the family?
   a. a notice   b. a painting   c. a map
2. How do the people in the family look?
   a. interested   b. bored   c. afraid

B. Find these words in your dictionary. Use them in the sentences.
   forecast   point   worry   cave
1. Don't go into that _____. There's a bear in there!
2. Everything will be okay. Please don't _____.
3. What's the weather _____ for tomorrow? Will it be sunny?
4. Where's the bird? I can't see it. Can you _____ to it for me?

C. Listen to Track 4 and answer these questions.
1. Who says, 'I'm hungry'?
   a. Olivia   b. Parker
2. Who is driving the car to the youth hostel?
   a. Chris   b. Frank
3. What kind of building is the youth hostel?
   a. an old building   b. a new building

After you read

COMPREHENSION
A. Circle the correct answers.
1. What is Parker's family name?
   a. Cwellyn   b. Wentworth   c. George
2. How many rooms do the family take in the youth hostel?
   a. two   b. three   c. four
3. What does Olivia ask George about?
   a. the kitchen   b. the ancient fort   c. walking up Snowdon
4. What does Parker say he wants to look for?
   a. an ancient fort   b. Merlin's cave
   c. a new path up Snowdon

B. Circle T for true or F for false for these sentences.
1. George never goes walking.   T / F
2. George says the Snowdon Ranger Path is dangerous.   T / F
3. The Snowdon Ranger Path goes to the top of Snowdon.   T / F
4. The Pyg Track goes to Pen-y-Pass.   T / F

C. Write short answers to these questions.
1. How long does it take to walk from the hostel to the top of Snowdon?
   _____

2. How long does it take to walk from the top of Snowdon to Pen-y-Pass?
   _____

3. How long does it take to drive from Dinas Emrys to Pen-y-Pass?
   _____

4. What is the name of the village George points to on the map?
   _____

D. Complete these sentences.
1. The family eats in the hostel's _____.
2. For dinner, Frank cooks the family a _____.
3. Olivia says tomorrow it will be sunny but _____.
4. Olivia will look at the weather forecast in the _____.

LANGUAGE ACTIVITIES
A. Match the words that go together in Chapter 2.
1. long   clothes
2. warm   walk
3. stone   jackets
4. rain   building

B. Write the missing vowels in these adjectives from Chapter 2.
1. _ sl _ _ p   3. _ _ sy
2. pr _ tty   4. h _ ngry

WHAT DO YOU THINK?
Frank says he is going to worry about Parker and Olivia on the mountain. Do you think he is right to worry? Why or why not?

_____

Chapter 3

Before you read

A. Look at the picture on page 16 and circle the correct answers.
1. Who do you think Olivia is talking to?
   a. two farmers   b. two walkers   c. two police officers
2. What can you see in the sky behind the mountains?
   a. a plane   b. birds   c. clouds

B. Find these words in your dictionary. Use them in the sentences.
   signal   summit   steep   careful
1. There is water on the floor. Be _____.
2. I can't go up the _____ hill on my bicycle. I'll walk up.
3. It's a long, hard climb to the _____ of the mountain.
4. I can't call for help. My phone has no _____.

C. Listen to Track 5 and answer these questions.
1. What time is it when Parker and Olivia are getting ready to go?
   a. five o'clock   b. nine o'clock
2. Who has the map and the phone?
   a. Olivia   b. Parker
3. Where will Parker and Olivia meet their parents?
   a. at the top of the mountain   b. at Pen-y-Pass

After you read

COMPREHENSION

A. Circle the correct answers.
1. What does Frank ask Parker and Olivia about?
   a. their shoes   b. warm clothing and food   c. the weather
2. What does George say about the weather?
   a. The forecast is okay, but the weather can change.
   b. It will be fine all day.   c. It will be stormy.
3. Where is the start of the track?
   a. across the road from the hostel   b. at Dinas Emrys
   c. at Pen-y-Pass
4. To find Merlin's cave, where does George tell Parker to look?
   a. to the north   b. to the west   c. to the south

B. Circle T for true or F for false for these sentences.
1. At first, the path goes up a hill and through some fields. T / F
2. Parker and Olivia stop and sit on a wall beside a gate. T / F
3. Two walkers say that a storm is coming. T / F
4. Parker and Olivia go down the path with the walkers. T / F

C. Complete these sentences.
1. At noon, there is a cold _____.
2. Parker tells Olivia it is time to go _____.
3. Olivia sees that her phone has no _____.
4. Parker and Olivia put on all their _____.

D. Write short answers to these questions.
1. When does the train bring people to the summit of Snowdon?
   _____
2. Is a train going to go up to the summit on this day?
   _____
3. What does Olivia say she and Parker can do on top of the mountain?
   _____
4. When the storm comes, what is it like for Parker and Olivia?
   _____

LANGUAGE ACTIVITIES
A. Write the correct prepositions in the spaces.
   to on through along
1. Parker and Olivia are _____ the Snowdon Ranger Path.
2. They walk _____ the track.
3. Olivia and Parker go _____ the gate.
4. They come _____ a railway line.

B. Use the letters to spell items of warm clothing from Chapter 3.
1. mjurpe _____   3. rafsc _____
2. anibee _____   4. lesogv _____

WHAT DO YOU THINK?
What would you do in Parker and Olivia's place? Would you keep going to the summit or would you go back down? Why?
_____

Chapters 4 and 5

Before you read

A. *Answer these questions about the story so far.*
1. Where is the storm now?
   a. over the Irish Sea   b. over Ireland   c. over Snowdonia
2. What can Parker and Olivia see when the storm comes?
   a. a view of lakes and forests   b. nothing but clouds
   c. the Irish Sea

B. *Find these words in your dictionary. Use them in the sentences.*
   marker   stairs   roar   flames
1. That house is on fire! Can you see the _____?
2. Let's walk down the _____ to the river.
3. I live near the zoo. At night I hear the lions _____.
4. There's a _____ on top of the highest hill on
   the island.

C. *Listen to Track 6 and answer these questions.*
1. What does Olivia say about storms on Snowdon?
   a. They always bring snow.   b. They come and go.
2. Who does Parker want to phone?
   a. Frank   b. George
3. What do they see at the summit?
   a. a stone marker   b. a seat

After you read

COMPREHENSION

A. *Circle the correct answers.*
1. Where does Parker say Y Lliwedd is?
   a. east of them   b. west of them   c. north of them
2. Where does Olivia say they can go to get out of the weather?
   a. to the stone marker   b. to the railway
   c. to the Visitors Centre
3. When Olivia slips on the ice, what does she hurt?
   a. her head   b. her foot   c. her hand
4. What does Parker give to Olivia before he walks off?
   a. his chocolate bar   b. a sandwich   c. some fruit and nuts

B. Circle T for true or F for false for these sentences.
1. In the storm, Parker calls to Merlin for help.   T / F
2. Merlin comes to Parker on the mountain.   T / F
3. A dragon comes and hurts Parker with hot flames.   T / F
4. The dragon makes the snow melt.   T / F

C. Complete these sentences.
1. The dragon roars, and flames shoot out of its _____.
2. Olivia tells Parker there are no such things as _____.
3. Parker carries the two _____.
4. They don't walk fast because the ground is still

_____.

D. Write short answers to these questions.
1. Why do Parker and Olivia want to get into the Visitors Centre? Give two reasons.

_____

2. How does Parker get into the Visitors Centre?

_____

3. Who answers the phone when Parker calls?

_____

4. What do Parker and Olivia eat in the Visitors Centre?

_____

LANGUAGE ACTIVITIES
A. Match the words that go together in Chapters 4 and 5.
1. take   your eyes
2. take   a window
3. break   photographs
4. close   a step

B. Write the missing vowels in these adjectives from Chapters 4 and 5.
1. w _ rm   3. fr_ _ z _ ng
2. h _ t   4. c _ ld

WHAT DO YOU THINK?
Is the dragon real? Does a dragon really come and help Parker – or is Parker just 'seeing things'? Do you agree with Parker or Olivia about the dragon? What would you *like* to be true?

Glossary

adj. adjective; *adv.* adverb; *n.* noun; *pron.* pronoun; *v.* verb

ahead of /ə'hed əv/ *adv.*	vor
already /ɔːl'redi/ *adv.*	schon
ancient /'eɪnʃ(ə)nt/ *adj.*	sehr alt, historisch
anything /'eni̯θɪŋ/ *pron.*	etwas; alles
archaeologist /ˌɑːki'ɒlədʒɪst/ *n.*	Archäologe, -in
back /bæk/ *adv.*	zurück
backpack /'bæk͵pæk/ *n.*	Rucksack
beard /bɪəd/ *n.*	Bart
break /breɪk/ *v.*	brechen
car park /'kɑː ͵pɑːk/ *n.*	Parkplatz
careful /'keəfl/ *adj.*	vorsichtig
cave /keɪv/ *n.*	Höhle
change /tʃeɪndʒ/ *v.*	sich ändern
circle /'sɜːkl/ *n.*	Kreis
curry /'kʌri/ *n.*	Currygericht
dig /dɪg/ *v.*	graben
dragon /'drægən/ *n.*	Drache
fight /faɪt/ *v.*	kämpfen
flame /fleɪm/ *n.*	Flamme
forecast /'fɔːkɑːst/ *n.*	Vorhersage
fort /fɔːt/ *n.*	Festung
freeze /friːz/ *v.*	gefrieren; erfrieren
gate /geɪt/ *n.*	Gatter, Tor
help /help/ *n.*	Hilfe
hill /hɪl/ *n.*	Hügel
icy /'aɪsi/ *adj.*	vereist
jumper /'dʒʌmpə/ *n.*	Pullover
kill /kɪl/ *v.*	töten
knight /naɪt/ *n.*	Ritter
long /lɒŋ/ *adj.*	lang

map /mæp/ *n.*	Landkarte
marker /ˈmɑːkə/ *n.*	Wegmarkierung
maybe /ˈmeɪbi/ *adv.*	vielleicht
melt /melt/ *v.*	schmelzen
mist /mɪst/ *n.*	Nebel
mountain /ˈmaʊntɪn/ *n.*	Berg
path /pɑːθ/ *n.*	Weg, Pfad
phone /fəʊn/ *n.*	Telefon
v.	anrufen
pick up /ˌpɪk ˈʌp/ *v.*	aufheben
point /pɔɪnt/ *v.*	zeigen
roar /rɔː/ *v.*	brüllen, tosen
safe /seɪf/ *adj.*	sicher
signal /ˈsɪgn(ə)l/ *n.*	Empfang
slip /slɪp/ *v.*	ausrutschen
smile /smaɪl/ *v.*	lächeln
stay /steɪ/ *v.*	bleiben
steep /stiːp/ *adj.*	steil
storm /stɔːm/ *n.*	Unwetter
summit /ˈsʌmɪt/ *n.*	Gipfel
that way /ˈðæt ˌweɪ/ *adv.*	dort (entlang)
track /træk/ *n.*	Weg
view /vjuː/ *n.*	Sicht, Aussicht
Visitors Centre /ˈvɪzɪtəz ˈsentə/ *n.*	Besucherzentrum
watch /wɒtʃ/ *v.*	beobachten
welcome /ˈwelkəm/ *adj.*	willkommen
wild /waɪld/ *adj.*	wild
without /wɪðˈaʊt/ *prep.*	ohne
wizard /ˈwɪzəd/ *n.*	Zauberer
worry /ˈwʌri/ *v.*	sich Sorgen machen
youth hostel /ˈjuːθ ˌhɒstl/ *n.*	Jugendherberge

Merlin's Dragon
Answer Key

Chapter 1
Before you read
A. 1. b, 2. a B. 1. fort,
2. ancient, 3. map, 4. dragon
C. 1. b, 2. a, 3. a

After you read
Comprehension
A. 1. b, 2. c, 3. b, 4. a B. 1. T, 2. F,
3. T, 4. T C. 1. king, 2. fall down,
3. wizard, 4. Emrys
D. 1. to kill a boy with no father,
2. two dragons, 3. *The dragons fight*,
4. the red dragon

Language activities
A. 1. walk across a bridge, 2. walk up a
hill, 3. look at a map, 4. climb over a
wall
B. 1. stories, 2. magic, 3. father,
4. Wales

What do you think?
Students' own answers

Chapter 2
Before you read
A. 1. c, 2. a B. 1. cave, 2. worry,
3. forecast, 4. point C. 1. b, 2. b, 3. a

After you read
Comprehension
A. 1. b, 2. a, 3. c, 4. b B. 1. F, 2. F,
3. T, 4. T C. 1. three or four hours,
2. three hours, 3. fifteen minutes,
4. Beddgelert
D. 1. kitchen, 2. curry, 3. cold,
4. morning

Language activities
A. 1. long walk, 2. warm clothes,
3. stone building, 4. rain jackets
B. 1. asleep, 2. pretty, 3. easy,
4. hungry

What do you think?
Students' own answers

Chapter 3
Before you read
A. 1. b, 2. c B. 1. careful, 2. steep,
3. summit, 4. signal
C. 1. b, 2. a, 3. b

After you read
Comprehension
A. 1. b, 2. a, 3. a, 4. c B. 1. T, 2. T,
3. T, 4. F C. 1. wind, 2. back,
3. signal, 4. warm clothes
D. 1. in the summer, 2. no,
3. eat lunch, 4. It's freezing; they can't
see anything five metres away.

Language activities
A. 1. on, 2. along, 3. through, 4. to
B. 1. jumper, 2. beanie, 3. scarf,
4. gloves

What do you think?
Students' own answers

Chapters 4 and 5
Before you read
A. 1. c, 2. b B. 1. flames,
2. stairs, 3. roar, 4. marker
C. 1. b, 2. a, 3. a

After you read
Comprehension
A. 1. a, 2. c, 3. b, 4. a B. 1. T, 2. F,
3. F, 4. T C. 1. mouth, 2. dragons,
3. backpacks, 4. icy
D. 1. to get out of the cold / out of the
bad weather; to find a phone / make a
phone call, 2. He breaks a window.
3. Chris, 4. their sandwiches

Language activities
A. 1. take photographs, 2. take a step,
3. break a window, 4. close your eyes
B. 1. warm, 2. hot, 3. freezing, 4. cold

What do you think?
Students' own answers